SHARKS
& OTHER OCEAN PREDATORS

Written by Gordon Volke
Illustrations by Sara Lees
and Mike Atkinson

TOP THAT! Kids™

Copyright © 2004 Top That! Publishing plc
Tide Mill Way, Woodbridge, Suffolk, IP12 1AP, UK
Top That! Kids is a Trademark of
Top That! Publishing plc
All rights reserved

OCEAN PREDATORS

Twenty thousand leagues under the sea... for real! Jules Verne wrote his famous story about a journey to the depths of the ocean, in 1874. It was a work of science fiction. Today, modern technology has turned his underwater adventure into scientific fact – and the results are even more exciting! Stand by to find out what it's really like to journey to the bottom of the sea...

What is an Ocean?

There are many seas in the world, but only four oceans. They are the Atlantic, the Pacific, the Indian and the Arctic. Oceans are very much bigger than seas. The Pacific is the largest and the deepest. The Atlantic is second largest and the Indian is the second deepest. The Arctic is the smallest, the most shallow and also the coldest!

Watery World

Oceans cover nearly three-quarters of Earth's surface. If you could pour all the water in the world into 100 equal tanks, 97 of them would be filled with water from the four oceans!

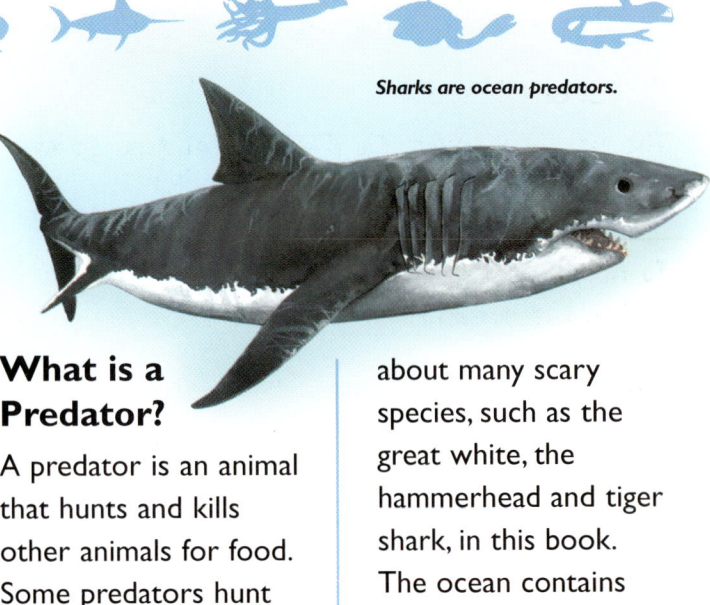

Sharks are ocean predators.

What is a Predator?

A predator is an animal that hunts and kills other animals for food. Some predators hunt alone; others hunt in packs. They all trap live prey with speed,

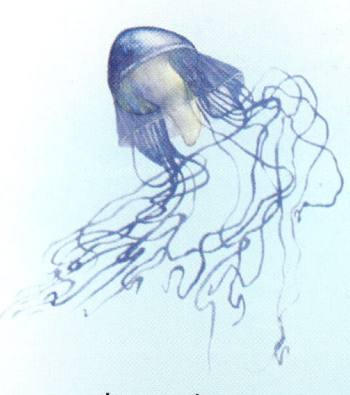

strength, cunning or poison. The shark is perhaps the best known of all the ocean predators, and you will be able to read about many scary species, such as the great white, the hammerhead and tiger shark, in this book. The ocean contains other predators, like jellyfish, which rely on toxins to paralyse their victims. Many, such as the octopus, use disguise and camouflage to catch their prey. Whichever way they operate, sea predators all have to kill in order to survive themselves.

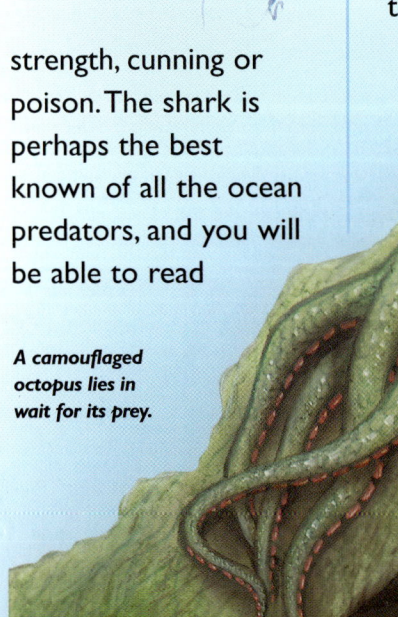

A camouflaged octopus lies in wait for its prey.

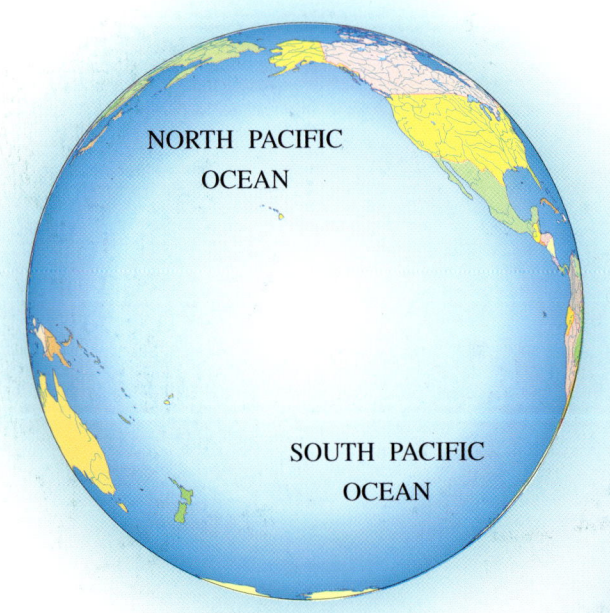

NORTH PACIFIC OCEAN

SOUTH PACIFIC OCEAN

Different Levels

The ocean changes the deeper you dive down into it. As a result, different types of underwater creatures live at different depths. To help in the study of these animals, scientists divide the ocean into four main zones.

The Epipelagic Zone

They start with the epipelagic zone, also known as the sunlit zone. It goes from the surface to 200 m down.

The Mesopelagic Zone

The next layer down is the mesopelagic zone. It's commonly known as the twilight zone and reaches 200 to 1,000 m down. Then we reach the bathypelagic zone. Known as the midnight zone; it reaches 1,000 to 4,000 m down.

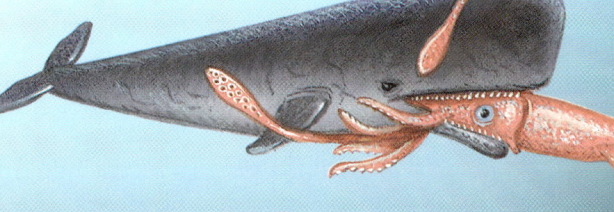

The Abyssopelagic Zone

Finally, we reach the abyssopelagic zone, and at 4,000 m to 6,000 m in depth, you can see why it is sometimes called the abyss (meaning 'nothing'). The average depth of the oceans is 3,650 m, so most of the time there are only three zones above the sea bed. The abyss is only found in certain places... and there is an even deeper level. It's called the hadalpelagic zone. This exists in one place – the Mariana Trench in the Pacific Ocean. Reaching a depth of 10,920 m, it is the deepest place in the world.

HERE'S HOW THE BOOK WORKS!

There are 24 pages in this book, all about different types of predators that can be found in the ocean's various zones. There are fantastic illustrations to bring the book alive – but you'll also notice that there are some blank spaces, too!

Don't worry! This is where you need to use the fabulous Stickertastic stickers – which are in the middle of the book. When you read about a particular fish, whale, crustacean, whatever... match the description to the Stickertastic sticker. Then simply put the sticker in the space to complete the scene. By the time you reach the end of each section, your head will be crammed full of information. You will also have a great picture to remind you of what you have just learned. In fact, you will be a Stickertastic Ocean Predators expert!

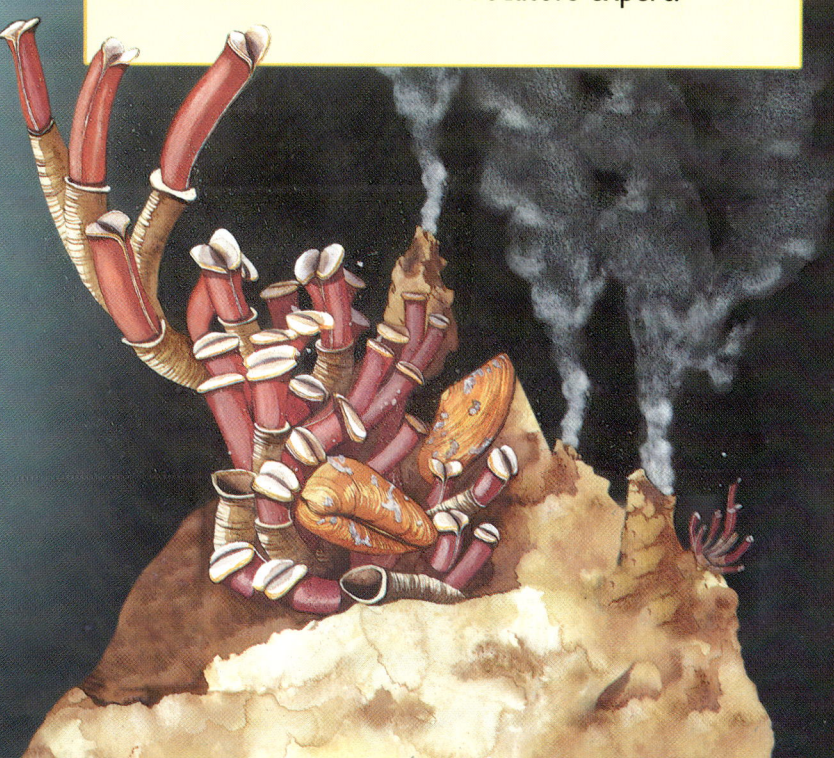

THE EPIPELAGIC ZONE – SUNLIGHT… AND SHARP TEETH!

Light from the sun penetrates to a depth of about 200 m below the surface of the sea. This makes everything clearly visible, so this level is also known as the sunlit zone. The water is also much warmer than that further down. This area under the surface of the ocean is teeming with life… and predators!

Killer Whale

This small, black and white whale, often called an orca, is actually the largest member of the dolphin family! It's a ferocious hunter, usually working in a pack. It will attack and eat anything, even huge whales, but tends to leave humans alone.

Plankton

Plankton

The light and warmth of the upper ocean allow billions of tiny sea plants and animals to breed. They are called plankton. Huge masses of plankton drift across the ocean like giant clouds, providing food for many much larger creatures.

Blue Whale

This gigantic mammal is the biggest animal in the world. It's about 30 m long and weighs a massive 150 tonnes! Its teeth, called baleen, are long, thin plates that filter plankton and tiny shrimps, known as krill, like a gigantic sieve.

Krill

Swordfish

This enormous fish, over 4 m long and weighing 450 kg, has no teeth for biting its prey. Instead, it has a long, pointed sword extending from its snout which it uses to slash and wound other fish which it then swallows.

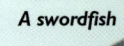
A swordfish

Great Barracuda

About 2 m long, this slim and powerful predator has two long rows of razor-sharp teeth. Found in the Atlantic and Pacific, it feeds on many types of fish. Bold and aggressive, it has been known to attack humans.

A killer whale

A swordfish

A blue whale

A bottlenose dolphin

A great barracuda

A sea lion

A manta ray

Sawfish

This strange-looking creature is actually a ray. It has a long, pointed snout edged with pointed teeth, like a saw, from which it gets its name. It uses this long, sharp probe to root out fish and other creatures living on the sea bed.

Sea Lion

Just like the dolphin, this creature is not usually thought of as a predator… but it is. It's a sleek, powerful swimmer which hunts fish, squid and octopus. It breeds in huge colonies along the seashore.

Bottlenose Dolphin

It's easy to forget that this friendly, intelligent animal is a predator, but it has many sharp teeth and catches fish in massive quantities! Dolphins live in groups called pods and communicate with each other by clicks and whistles.

Manta Ray

Often called the devil fish, this huge creature glides along near the surface like a massive underwater bird. It feeds on plankton that it sweeps into its wide open mouth. Sometimes, manta ray leap right out of the water and make a very loud splash.

THE MESOPELAGIC ZONE – DARK, COLD... AND DEADLY!

Below 200 m, this zone is too dark for plants to survive. The creatures living at these depths have to feed on dead material floating down from above... or each other! Little light can reach the murky waters, which is why this level is commonly known as the twilight zone. Unsurprisingly, it has its fair share of powerful killers.

Sperm Whale

The sperm whale eats giant squid and is able to dive right to the bottom of this zone and into the next in search of prey. Measuring up to 20 m in length, it is blue-grey or brown – but is occasionally white, like the whale in the story *Moby Dick*.

A giant squid

I Spied a Sea Spider!

This huge, delicate creature lives on the sea bed when it exists at this level. It has four pairs of thin legs which span over 60 cm, allowing the spider to walk along the ocean floor without getting entangled or causing a stir.

A sea spider

Giant Squid

The giant squid is the largest animal in the world without a backbone. It has ten arms, known as tentacles, which can grow up to 14 m long! It's a shy, secretive creature which has been caught but never filmed living underwater.

Gulper Eel

The gulper is a soft-bodied fish with a thin tail up to 2 m long. It's a remarkable creature because of its huge mouth and extending

A gulper eel

stomach that allows it to catch, swallow and digest very large prey.

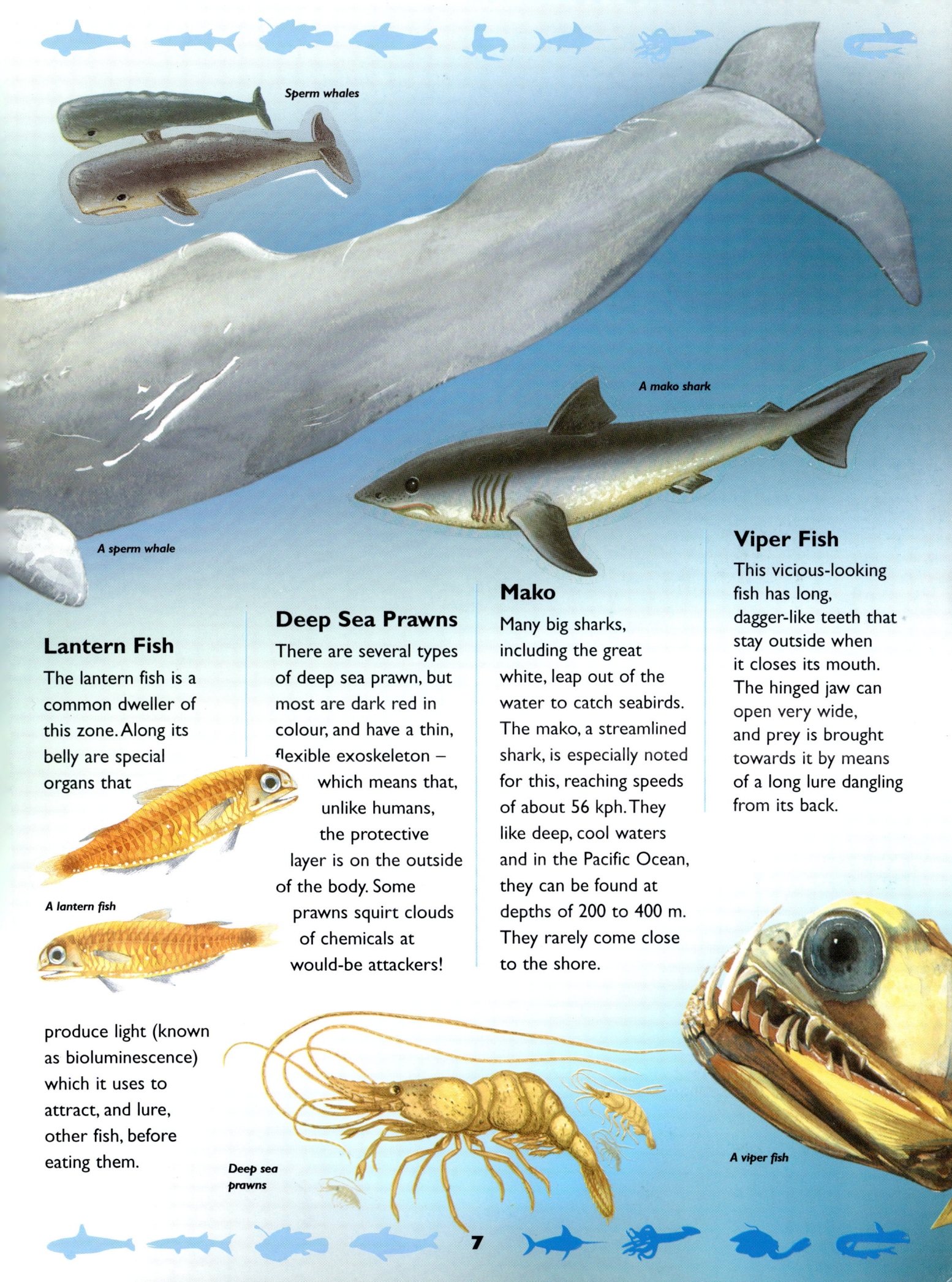

Sperm whales

A mako shark

A sperm whale

Lantern Fish

The lantern fish is a common dweller of this zone. Along its belly are special organs that

A lantern fish

Deep Sea Prawns

There are several types of deep sea prawn, but most are dark red in colour, and have a thin, flexible exoskeleton – which means that, unlike humans, the protective layer is on the outside of the body. Some prawns squirt clouds of chemicals at would-be attackers!

Mako

Many big sharks, including the great white, leap out of the water to catch seabirds. The mako, a streamlined shark, is especially noted for this, reaching speeds of about 56 kph. They like deep, cool waters and in the Pacific Ocean, they can be found at depths of 200 to 400 m. They rarely come close to the shore.

Viper Fish

This vicious-looking fish has long, dagger-like teeth that stay outside when it closes its mouth. The hinged jaw can open very wide, and prey is brought towards it by means of a long lure dangling from its back.

produce light (known as bioluminescence) which it uses to attract, and lure, other fish, before eating them.

Deep sea prawns

A viper fish

BATHYPELAGIC ZONE – THE INKY DEPTHS

Below 1,000 m, there is no light at all. It's a completely black world, so this level is commonly known as the midnight zone. The water is bitterly cold and the pressure here is enormous. You might imagine that no life could exist in such an unfriendly environment, but you would be wrong…

Darkness and Light

Most of the fish living at these depths are as black as the water that they swim in. This makes them almost impossible to see and keeps them safe from predators. Light organs have to be used to catch prey or attract a mate.

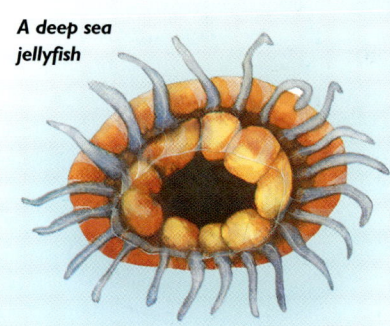

A deep sea jellyfish

Deep Sea Jellyfish

Dark red in colour, this jellyfish is tough, like bendy rubber. As do other jellyfish, it uses long, stinging tentacles to catch its prey. It also has a special gland which throws out a dazzling blue light when attacked.

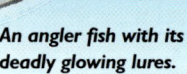

An angler fish with its deadly glowing lures.

Angler Fish

A remarkable fish which has a glowing light on the end of a line to lure prey to its gaping jaws. The teeth slant backwards, so nothing can escape. Its stomach expands to digest large meals.

A whipnose

Whipnose

A small, hunter from the depths of the Atlantic and Pacific, the whipnose uses the same technique as the angler fish – but with a much longer line. It uses this to lure the prey nearer and nearer to its mouth… and then strikes!

Megamouth Shark

It has existed for millions of years, but nobody knew about it until one was caught near Hawaii in 1976. Nearly 5 m long, this slow-swimming shark has a gigantic mouth that actually glows in the dark!

Lancet Fish

This thin fish has lightweight bones and very little muscle which make it easier to move around in the extreme water pressure. The huge, sail-like fin on its back can be raised and lowered. The lancet fish eats squid and hatchet fish.

A lancet fish

Gigantura

Despite being long and thin, this fish can stretch its stomach to digest a large catch. It has unusual eyes that look like binoculars. They allow it to pick up the tiniest speck of light from other creatures.

A megamouth shark

A gigantura

THE ABYSSOPELAGIC ZONE – VOYAGE TO THE BOTTOM OF THE SEA

Many of the creatures from the midnight zone are also found in the abyss, which comes from a Greek word meaning 'no bottom'. In addition, there are other bizarre-looking life forms that have all found clever ways to survive in this most hostile of environments.

An umbrella mouth gulper

Rat Tail

The most common deep-sea fish, that is more properly called a grenadier. All 300 species have long, thin, rat-like tails – hence their name. It has huge eyes for seeing in the dark and an extended snout for rooting around the sea bed for food.

A rat tail

Sea Snails

This creature is actually a fish and is often called a snailfish. It looks like a giant tadpole with its rounded head and long tail fin. Many of the 115 species have a suction disk below their heads to attach themselves to the sea bed.

Tripod Fish

A tripod is a three-legged instrument or item of furniture. The fish gets its name from its three long, thin fins – one at the back and two at the front. It uses these to detect prey scuttling about on the sea bed.

A tripod fish

Sea snails

Umbrella Mouth Gulper

This weird-looking eel, with its high-curving tail that picks up vibrations in the water from approaching prey, swims with its mouth open all the time. It swallows shrimps, small fish and anything else as it scours the ocean depths like a vacuum cleaner!

A stalked crinoid

Stalked Crinoid

A plant-like animal, and relative of the brittle star, it grows out of the sea bed like a giant feathery hand. Each crinoid has several waving tentacles lined with special hairs that sweep food towards the creature's ever-open mouth.

Mysteries of the Deep

As modern technology allows us to explore further and deeper than ever before, new

species of marine life are being discovered all the time. Who knows what other kinds of weird and wonderful sea creatures are lurking deep beneath the waves? In 1960, two marine scientists, called Jacques Piccard and Donald Walsh, descended to the bottom of the Mariana Trench. They used an immensely strong diving chamber called *Trieste* that could withstand the huge water pressure at this vast depth.

SHARKS – THE TEETH OF THE SEA

Les Dents De La Mer – the teeth of the sea – this is the French translation of the film title *Jaws*. It is a very good description of sharks, the ocean's most aggressive and plentiful predators. Stand by to fill the next four pages with some of these deadly fish!

Thresher Shark

This shark has a very long tail, up to 3 m long. The thresher swims through a shoal of small fish, like herring or pilchard, swishing its tail. This stuns lots of fish which the shark then returns to and eats.

A thresher shark

Great White

This is the biggest, fiercest and most famous shark of them all. Over 7 m long and weighing as much as an elephant, this shark has over 50 jagged teeth. Its favourite food is a seal, but it will attack anything, including humans. It stays mainly in the shallower parts of coastal temperate waters, but sometimes makes dives into the midnight zone.

Basking Shark

Like the whale shark, the basking shark is a slow-swimming, plankton feeder found near the surface of the Atlantic, Pacific and Indian Oceans. It is almost as big as its cousin, growing to a length of about 14 m.

A basking shark

Ramoras

Whale Shark

This is the biggest member of the shark family and the largest fish in the world. It grows to a staggering 15 m long! The whale shark is a gentle creature, swimming just under the surface and feeding on plankton and krill. Whale sharks have around 3,000 teeth but these are all very tiny and not used much. This is because they feed by swimming with their mouths open, taking in huge amounts of seawater and any small creatures in it.

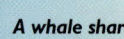
A whale shark

Hitching a Ride

Many large sharks carry passengers called ramoras. These small fish have a sucker on their head which they use to hitch a ride. Pilot fish also like to travel close to sharks because they know other predators won't come near and attack them.

Killing with their Eyes Closed

When sharks attack their prey, there is a danger they will get injured in the struggle. So, to protect their eyes, sharks have a special layer of skin, called a nictitating membrane, that slides down over the eyes like a shutter.

A shark's eye

A great white shark

Tiger Shark

The tiger gets its name from the striped markings on its back. Young tiger sharks have spots, which grow together to form stripes as they get older. Not quite as big or heavy as the great white, the tiger shark is equally ferocious. It eats almost anything – fish, seals, dolphins, squid and even other sharks, as well as stingray and sea snakes. Its teeth grow all the time, replacing those that break or fall out.

White Tipped Reef Shark

This shark is special because it likes to sleep during the day and hunt atnight. Often found together in caves, reef sharks go their separate ways when it gets dark and hunt fish, crabs, lobsters and octopus.

A white tipped reef shark

A tiger shark

SHARKS

Sharks have been swimming in our oceans for millions of years. They will have to continue doing so as well because sharks cannot breathe unless they move forwards. The moment that they stop swimming, they drown.

Blue Shark

A blue shark

This shark is a great long-distance swimmer. It is known to travel between 2,000 and 3,000 km in search of a mate. One tagged blue shark was recorded travelling nearly 6,000 km from South to North America.

A saw shark

Saw Shark

Most sharks have sharp teeth inside their mouths, but the saw shark has them outside as well! They are situated along each side of a very long snout. Like the sawfish, it uses this to stir up the sea bed to find prey to eat.

Sleeper Shark

Not all sharks live in warm oceans. The sleeper shark is found in the icy waters of the Arctic Ocean. It eats fish, seals, small whales, crabs and any edible rubbish thrown away from human settlements on the shore! Sleeper sharks even hunt giant squid as their prey.

A sleeper shark

Bull Shark

Most sharks live in the ocean where the water is salty. Not the bull shark! This large killer is able to live in fresh water for several weeks at a time, so it swims up rivers. One was found in the Amazon, about 3,000 km from the coast!

Hammerhead Shark

Hammerhead sharks are so-called because of their distinctive head shape. Their eyes are positioned at either end of the 'hammer' which enables them to easily spot their prey.

A hammerhead shark

Leopard Shark

The leopard shark is so named because its markings of dark brown spots are like those of a leopard. It is also able to change its colour to adapt to its environment. This acts as a form of camouflage so that it can hide among areas of coral, a good source of food, and rock. Its spots start to fade as it reaches adulthood when it needs less protection from its predators.

A leopard shark

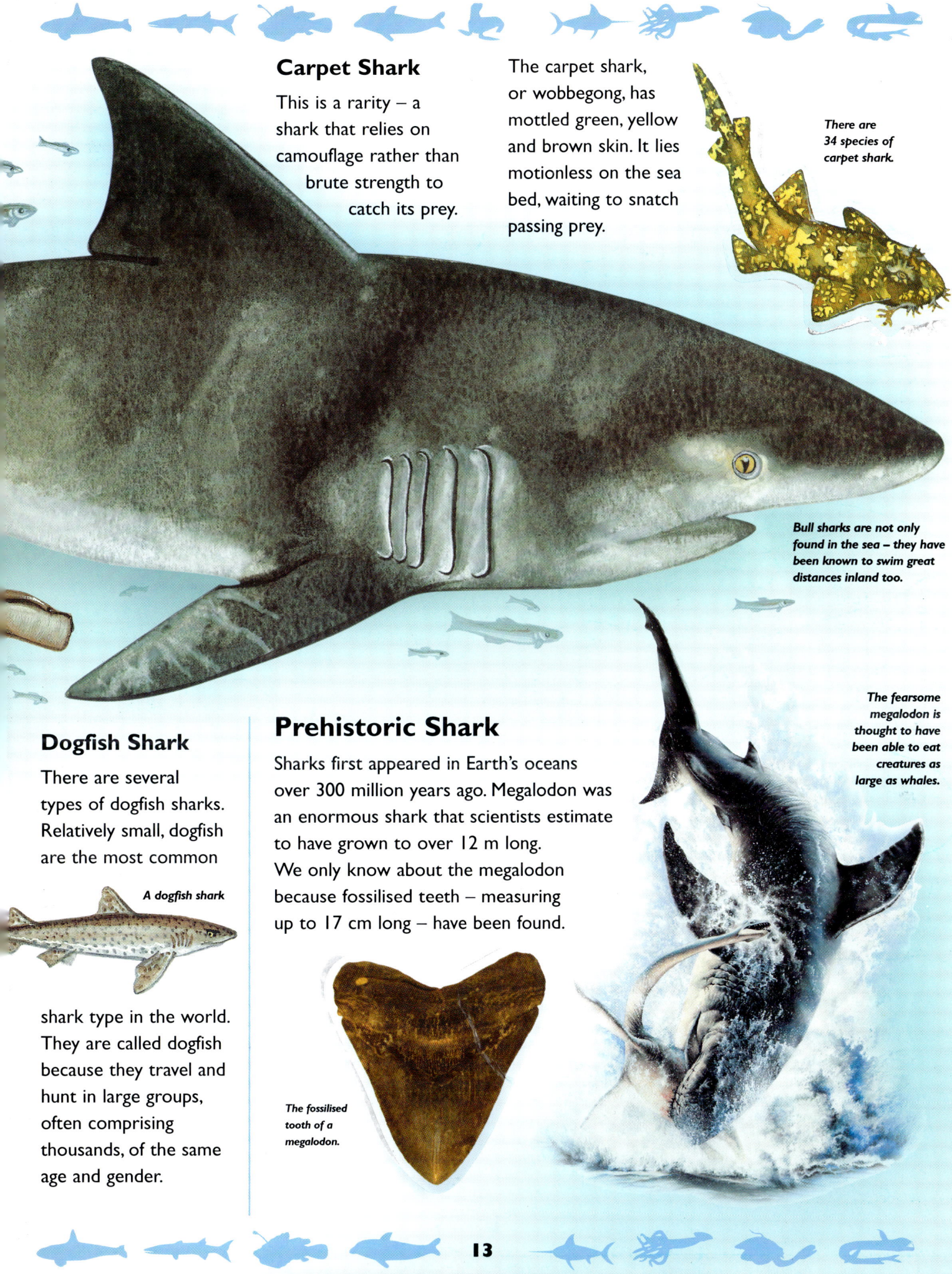

Carpet Shark

This is a rarity – a shark that relies on camouflage rather than brute strength to catch its prey. The carpet shark, or wobbegong, has mottled green, yellow and brown skin. It lies motionless on the sea bed, waiting to snatch passing prey.

There are 34 species of carpet shark.

Bull sharks are not only found in the sea – they have been known to swim great distances inland too.

Dogfish Shark

There are several types of dogfish sharks. Relatively small, dogfish are the most common

A dogfish shark

shark type in the world. They are called dogfish because they travel and hunt in large groups, often comprising thousands, of the same age and gender.

Prehistoric Shark

Sharks first appeared in Earth's oceans over 300 million years ago. Megalodon was an enormous shark that scientists estimate to have grown to over 12 m long. We only know about the megalodon because fossilised teeth – measuring up to 17 cm long – have been found.

The fossilised tooth of a megalodon.

The fearsome megalodon is thought to have been able to eat creatures as large as whales.

ANATOMY OF A SHARK

Sharks can vary greatly in their appearance, size and colour. However, there are some features that are common to most species. Their bodies are streamlined, they have rigid fins and flexible, powerful tails – to assist their movement through the water.

Blood and Water

The shark breathes through its gills, found on the insides of the gill slits and visible on the outside of the body. Water is taken in through the mouth, and runs in the opposite direction to the way blood runs to the gills. This allows the shark to mix more oxygen into the bloodstream.

Fins

Most sharks have two dorsal fins to help them maintain balance – the rear one is normally smaller. A pelvic fin helps to keep the shark upright. Male sharks have reproductive organs here, called claspers.

Jaws of Teeth

Some sharks use their jaws and sharp teeth to rip up prey, while others, known as filter feeders, simply swim with their mouths open, eating anything that swims inside. Sharks' teeth vary between different species, depending on the fish they eat – curved for slippery fish or serrated for bony fish.

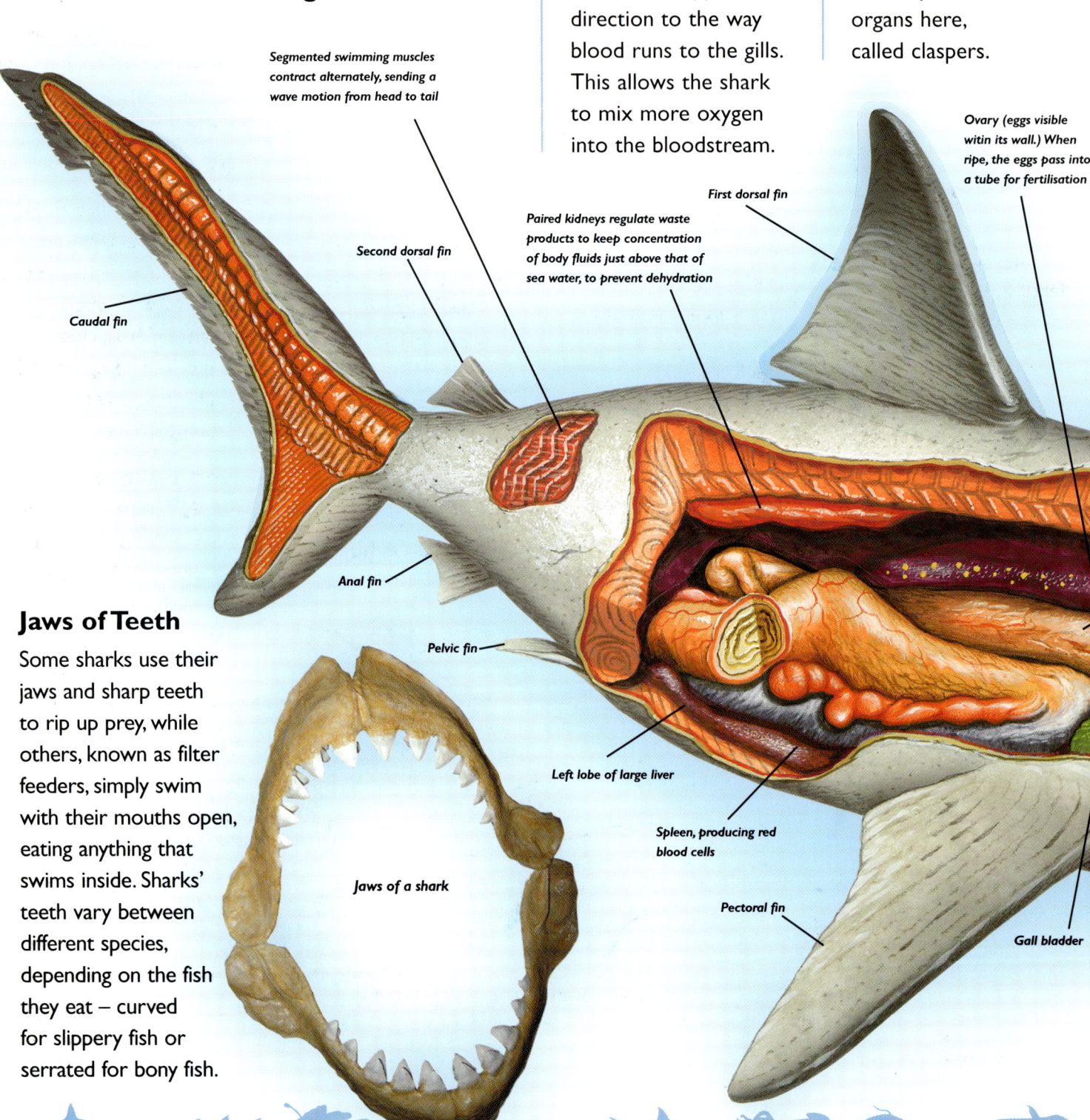

Segmented swimming muscles contract alternately, sending a wave motion from head to tail

Caudal fin

Second dorsal fin

Anal fin

Paired kidneys regulate waste products to keep concentration of body fluids just above that of sea water, to prevent dehydration

First dorsal fin

Ovary (eggs visible witin its wall.) When ripe, the eggs pass into a tube for fertilisation

Pelvic fin

Jaws of a shark

Left lobe of large liver

Spleen, producing red blood cells

Pectoral fin

Gall bladder

Bendy Backbones

Altogether, there are 370 different species of shark. They all have one thing in common – they don't have a hard, bony skeleton. Instead, it is made of a bendy material called 'cartilage'. This makes sharks excellent swimmers.

Making Babies

All sharks reproduce by internal fertilisation. The male's claspers transfer sperm into the female. Viviparous sharks give birth to up to 100 live young, called pups. Oviparous sharks lay eggs that attach to rocks and hatch after six to fifteen months. Ovoviviparous sharks grow young in an egg inside the female's body. The egg hatches inside the female.

The laterial line of a shark

SENSES

Vision
Sharks' eyes are very sensitive to light and can find some things in dark, murky water.

Taste
Their taste buds are on bumps inside their mouths. They will spit out anything that isn't tasty.

Smell
A shark's sense of smell is its most useful and highly developed sense. They can detect very weak smells in huge amounts of water.

Touch
They can feel things with their nose – some have feelers, called barbels, that they use to find things buried in the sea bed.

Bio Compass
It is thought that sharks which travel thousands of miles use this sense to 'tune in' to Earth's magnetic field. This 'biological compass' helps them to find their way around the oceans.

Sixth Sense
Sharks have a sixth sense. They have special pores on their heads called ampullae of Lorenzini. These pick up the very weak electrical signals produced by the muscles of living things in water.

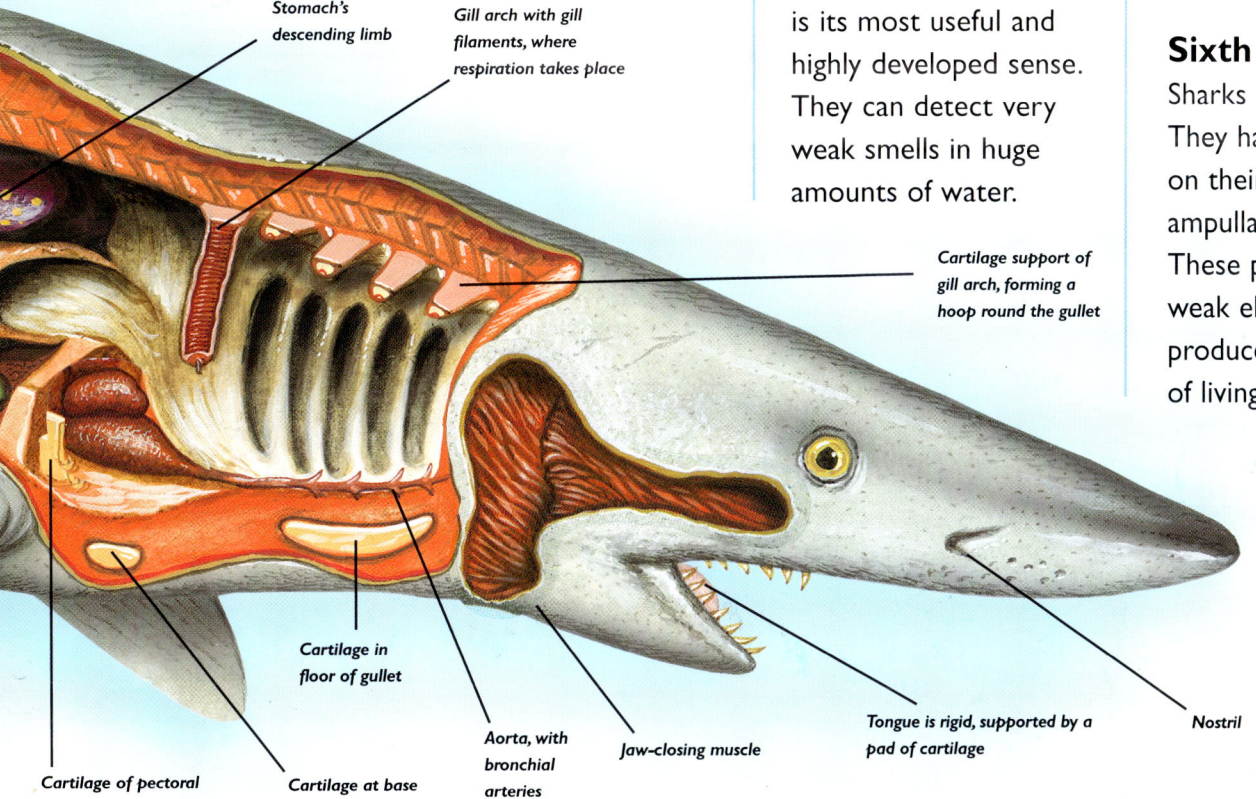

POISONOUS PREDATORS – THE KILLER TOUCH!

So you've read all about the big guys, but what else is out there? Many smaller ocean predators hunt in a very different way. They use poisonous venom to defend themselves or catch their prey. These toxins are very powerful – as any unlucky swimmer who has come into contact with them may tell you! Venomous sea creatures can cause agonising pain… and even death!

Sea Snake
This creature produces the most powerful toxin found anywhere in the world! Fortunately, most venomous sea snakes live far out in the Pacific Ocean where they like to swim together on the surface, basking in the warm sunshine.

A sea snake

Stingray
This cousin of the manta ray has a sting in its tale – literally! This creature likes to live in the warm, shallow water near the beach. If disturbed, it lashes out with its long, whip-like tail and injects venom into its attacker.

A stringray

A Portuguese man-of-war

Portuguese Man-of-war
This famous jellyfish, named after the fighting galleons of old, has tentacles up to 50 m long! They are equipped with stinging cells that paralyse passing fish. The creature's body is a gas-filled float and it moves along by raising a crest like a sail!

Lionfish
This beautiful-looking but deadly fish is found around coral reefs in tropical waters. Its spine is loaded with powerful venom which keeps attackers away, allowing the lionfish to swim gracefully past.

Stonefish
This ugly creature, found in tropical waters, is every swimmer's nightmare. It has the same skin colouring as the sea bed, so is almost impossible to spot. If you tread on one by accident, it raises it spines and injects an agonising dose of poison.

A stonefish

Cone Snail

This killer, which looks like a harmless shell, is found around coral reefs where it hunts at night. As a fish passes, the cone snail shoots out a single tooth loaded with venom. The paralysed prey is then sucked into the food tube and eaten.

A cone snail

Arrows of Death

Many poisonous sea predators have evolved barbed tips to their spines. This extra head on the sharp point acts like an arrowhead or a fishing hook – once inserted into a victim, it stays there and cannot be pulled out!

A lionfish

Sea Wasp

This transparent jellyfish, found off the coast of northern Australia, does more than sting like a wasp. Terrible pain is felt wherever its tentacles touch your skin, followed by breathing difficulties and death in a large number of cases.

Blue-ringed Octopus

The blue-ringed octopus is no larger than a golf ball, but its bite is lethal to humans. Usually brown or yellow, its bright blue rings only appear a few seconds before it delivers its fatal bite! The poison is contained in its saliva – each octopus has enough poison to kill over twenty people within minutes.

A sea wasp

A blue-ringed octopus

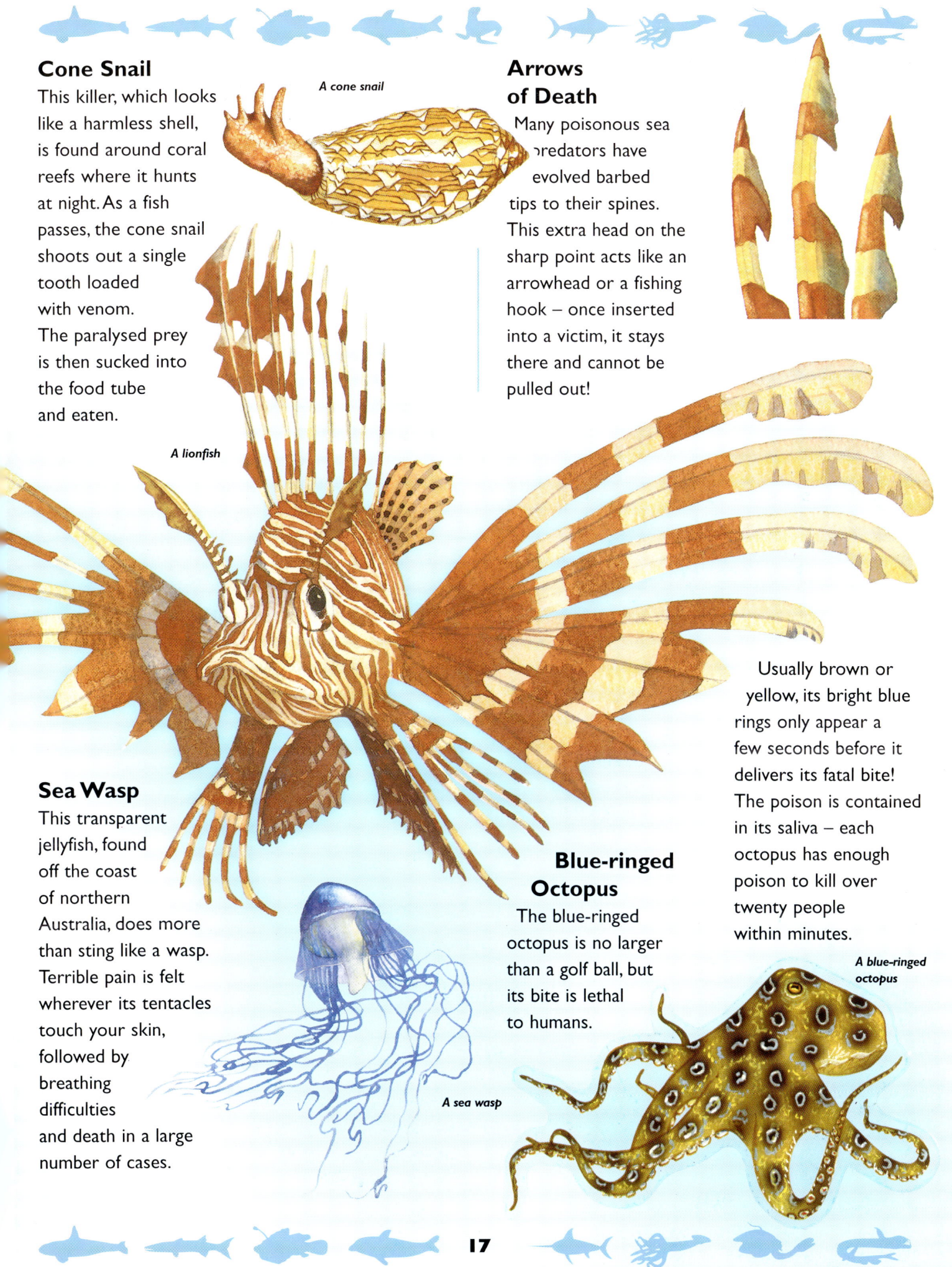

OCTOPUS, SQUID AND ALL ARMS AND LEGS!

Octopus and squid belong to a group of animals called cephalopods. These are also predators, but have no backbone or skeleton of any kind. Cephalopod means 'head-footed' – every member of the group has a head surrounded by tentacles. They are all clever predators who use disguise, cunning, speed and venom to catch their prey.

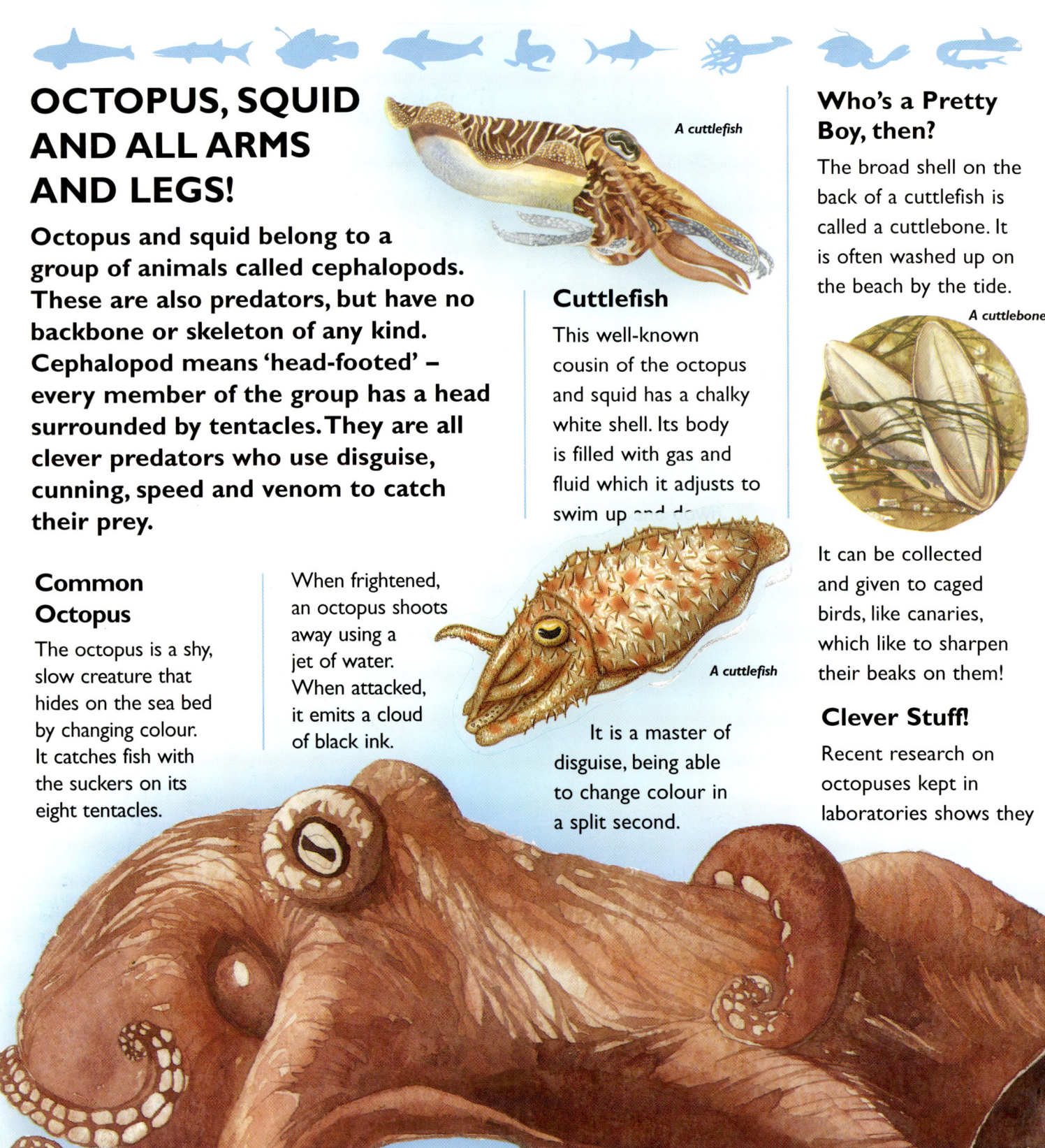

A cuttlefish

Cuttlefish

This well-known cousin of the octopus and squid has a chalky white shell. Its body is filled with gas and fluid which it adjusts to swim up and down.

A cuttlefish

It is a master of disguise, being able to change colour in a split second.

Who's a Pretty Boy, then?

The broad shell on the back of a cuttlefish is called a cuttlebone. It is often washed up on the beach by the tide.

A cuttlebone

It can be collected and given to caged birds, like canaries, which like to sharpen their beaks on them!

Clever Stuff!

Recent research on octopuses kept in laboratories shows they

Common Octopus

The octopus is a shy, slow creature that hides on the sea bed by changing colour. It catches fish with the suckers on its eight tentacles.

When frightened, an octopus shoots away using a jet of water. When attacked, it emits a cloud of black ink.

The strange-looking octopus has eight tentacles.

are highly intelligent creatures. They have good memories and quickly learn how to recognise coloured symbols or perform tasks to obtain food.

Spotted Octopus

Most types of octopus are harmless to humans, but this one is a deadly killer. It uses its poison to deter predators. However, if you are unlucky enough to be stung

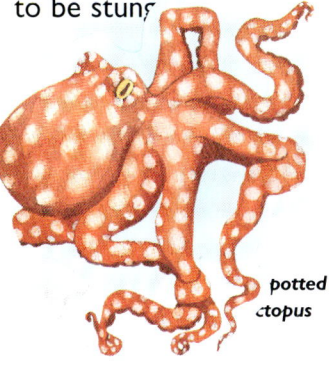

A spotted octopus

by one, you become paralysed and can slip into a coma which often leads to death.

Common Squid

Most of the time, squid swim backwards trailing their ten long tentacles behind them. In order to move

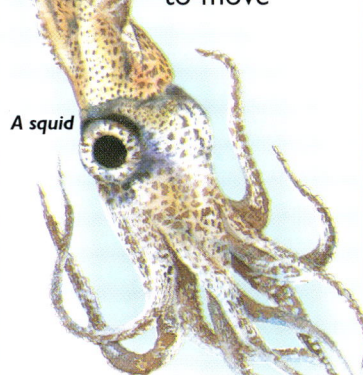

A squid

through the water it pumps water in and out of its body. When hunting, however, it swims forwards to grab its prey. The squid injects its victims with poison before tearing them to pieces with its beak-like jaws. The common squid is able to change colour within a few seconds.

Chambered Nautilus

Nautilus' live at great depths in the ocean – usually below 600 m. They move through the water in a similar way as squid, by forcing water through a movable siphon.

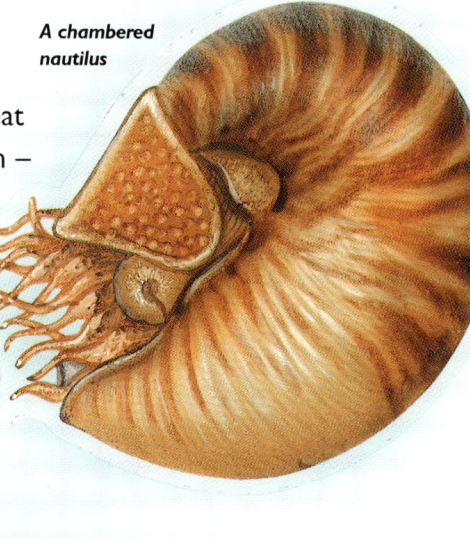

A chambered nautilus

A chambered nautilus changes to a shape resembling a torpedo as it moves through the water.

Its chambered shell acts as a form of buoyancy as well providing protection against its predators. They have around 90 tentacles but unlike those of the octopus, they do not have suckers attached to them. Their eyes work in the same way as a pinhole camera – a sharp image is made by narrowing their pupils.

Mimic Octopus

This small octopus has developed the art of disguise to perfection. When disturbed, the mimic octopus can change its shape and colouring to make itself look like a sea snake, a stingray or a lionfish – all threatening predators!

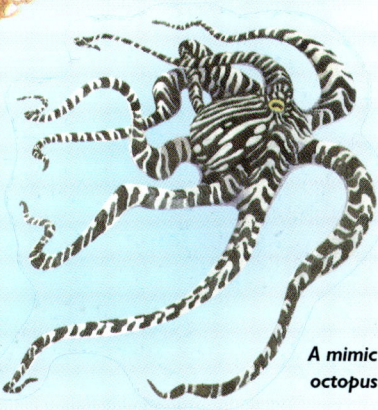

A mimic octopus

Giant Squid

Giant squid are the largest of all known cephalopods. They have long, torpedo-like bodies, five pairs of arms and a mouth that looks like a beak and can reach a total length of around 13 m although the longest recorded giant squid measured 18 m. Their eyes are huge and can reach a diameter of 45 cm! They are the prey of the sperm whale even though it can be as long as its predator.

CRUSTACEANS AND SEA BED INVERTEBRATES

The sea bed, covered with sand and colourful plants, looks like an underwater garden. Humans have dived to these depths and report it to be eerily quiet. However, appearances can be deceptive! The bottom of the ocean swarms with predators plying their deadly trade in many different ways and it is certainly a noisy hotbed of activity to those who dwell there...

Homes on the Sea Bed

Sunken ships and even the remains of crashed aircraft litter the sea bed in ever-increasing numbers. They bring danger and pollution, but many marine animals use them like caves and make their homes in them. Divers like to explore wrecks for the vast array of underwater creatures they attract.

A sea anemone

Sea Anemone

There are more than 1,000 types of sea anemone. The largest and most colourful are found in warm, tropical oceans. They have hundreds of waving arms with stinging cells that paralyse passing fish and other small marine animals.

Wrecks provide a home for much marine life.

A lobster

Lobster

Like the crab, the lobster is a member of the crustacean family which means 'body with a shell.' Its pincers are even bigger and stronger than a crab's. The lobster has ten legs altogether and is a dull brown colour. It only turns pink when it is caught and boiled.

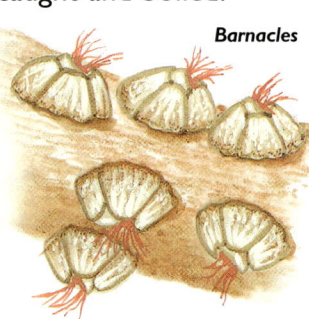

Barnacles

Barnacles

There are two types of barnacles found in Earth's oceans. The Acorn barnacles attach themselves directly to rock by their plates while goose barnacles are attached to the end of a stalk. They each have six pairs of long legs which they use to sweep through the sea water to filter plankton for food.

A crab

Place your crab sticker here.

Crab

There are many different species of crab. They live in oceans, rivers and lakes and sometimes even on land. They have powerful pincers on their front legs with which they can catch and hold their prey. Their other distinguishing feature is that they also have eyes on stalks that can be pulled into the shell for safety.

A spider crab

Giant Clam

There are over 12,000 different types of clam. This one is the biggest, measuring well over 1 metre across. Found on the bed of the Pacific and Indian Oceans, the giant clam shuts its powerful sides, trapping anything passing inside – including a swimmer's foot!

A giant clam

Spider Crab

Spider crabs live on sand and among rocks to a depth of no more than 50 m. They often place seaweed and sponge on their spiny backs to act as a form of camouflage. Hook-like hairs on its shell catch algae which remain attached to the shell.

A mantis shrimp

Mantis Srimp

Found in tropical waters, there are several species of mantis shrimp. They are carnivorous creatures and while some use their claws to spear their prey others use their claw as a club to smash their prey.

A sea slug

Sea Slugs

There are hundreds of species of sea slugs. It is the common name given to shell-less marine gastropods. Many do not look like the garden slugs we are familiar with, some being brightly coloured and delicately shaped.

Parrot Fish

This colourful fish gets its name from its beak which looks like that of a parrot. The beak is used to scrape tiny life forms called algae from the rocks of coral reefs. Parrot fish are quite big, growing to well over a 1 long.

A sea cucumber

Sea Cucumber

There are over 1,100 species of sea cucumber. Some have long, thin tentacles with sticky tips to catch prey. Others shoot out a poison that kills nearby creatures. This poison is not harmful to humans.

Many creatures live on, or near, coral reefs.

A parrot fish

The Crown of Thorn Starfish

Most starfish are relatively harmless. However, the 'crown of

A starfish

thorn' starfish usually preys on coral, and is a particular nuisance on the Great Barrier Reef in Australia.

ASSASSINS OF THE SEA WIND

The ultimate ocean predator… humans! American songwriter, John Stewart, once described whale hunters as 'assassins of the sea wind'. It's a perfect description of our attitude to the creatures of the sea. Whales, sharks and many species of fish are now in danger of extinction because they are being killed in too great a number.

Cod

The days of cod fish fingers and cod and chips from the fish and chip shop will soon be over. Stocks of this large Atlantic fish are at an all-time low. If cod continues to be overfished, they will not recover and will disappear forever.

Tuna

Skipjack tuna, yellowfin tuna and the massive bluefin tuna are just some species of tuna fish that are caught in their millions every year. A valuable source of healthy food, stocks are rapidly going down and they are becoming harder to find.

Blue Marlin

This enormous blue and silver fish with a long, sharp nose is a favourite target of deep-sea sports fishermen. It can weigh up to 450 kg, making it an exciting catch to struggle with and land.

Disappearing Coral

It is not only fish and sea-going mammals that are in danger from humans, the beautiful coral reefs are also under threat. Shells and coloured rocks are taken and sold as souvenirs to tourists visiting places like the Great Barrier Reef in Australia.

Dolphins in Danger

Many big fish and mammals are also caught by accident. The bluenose dolphin, for example, is no use to humans, but it is killed in large numbers as it gets caught up in fishing nets and drowns. Fortunately, new nets are being introduced to stop this happening.

Sand Shark

Also known as the sandtiger shark, this large ocean predator is found in both temperate and tropical oceans. They catch fish by using the long, sharp teeth located at the front of the mouth. It is typical of the 100 million sharks that are caught and killed every year. Sharks reproduce slowly, so they cannot keep up with the numbers being taken. Without sharks, the balance of life in the oceans will be ruined.

A sand shark

Right Whale

This whale got its name from the fact that it was the 'right one' to catch. A slow swimmer, it floats when it is killed. Like many other types of whale, the right whale is now scarce because so many have been killed by hunters.

Whales often become covered in barnacles.

Salmon

Here's a success story amidst all the doom and gloom. Instead of catching wild salmon all the time, many salmon farms are now providing this delicious fish for the supermarkets. Young fish are grown in special pens floating in the sea.

A salmon

THE FOOD CHAIN

You get energy from the food you eat. Similarly, all living creatures get energy from their food so that they can move and grow. Marine animals depend on each other for food. A food chain shows how each living thing gets its food.

TOP of the food chain

Top of the Food Chain
Millions of people all over the world, on every continent, depend on many species of fish for food. That's why it is so important that fish populations are conserved. However, overfishing by huge, modern fishing fleets is threatening the entire ocean food chain.

Sun Energy
The oceanic food chain begins with microscopic drifting plants called phytoplankton. These are creatures that gain much of their energy from the sun. Phytoplankton are eaten by small creatures called zooplankton which, in turn, are eaten by tiny animals such as crabs, jellyfish, corals and worms.

BOTTOM of the food chain

Fish Food
These creatures, in turn, become food for fish. Big fish eat smaller fish. At the top of the food chain are large predatory fish such as sharks, together with mammals such as sealions, as well as some species of seabirds. However, a very large fish, the whale shark, and some very large mammals, like the baleen whales, feed directly on zooplankton.